Animal Homes

Bears and Their Dens

grizzly bear cub

by Linda Tagliaferro

Consulting Editor: Gail Saunders-Smith, Ph.D.

Consultant: Klari Lea, President
American Bear Association
Orr, Minnesota

Capstone
press

Mankato, Minnesota

Pebble Plus is published by Capstone Press
151 Good Counsel Drive, P.O. Box 669, Mankato, Minnesota 56002
www.capstonepress.com

1 2 3 4 5 6 09 08 07 06 05 04

Library of Congress Cataloging-in-Publication Data
Tagliaferro, Linda.
    Bears and their dens / by Linda Tagliaferro.
    p. cm.—(Pebble Plus, animal homes)
    Summary: Simple text and photographs describe bears and the dens in which they live.
    Includes bibliographical references (p. 23) and index.
    ISBN 0-7368-2381-6 (hardcover)
    1. Bears—Juvenile literature. 2. Bears—Habitations—Juvenile literature. [1. Bears—Habitations.
2. Bears—Habits and behavior.]
I. Title. II. Series.
QL737.C27T325 2004
599.78—dc22   2003013422

Editorial Credits
Martha E. H. Rustad, editor; Linda Clavel, series designer; Deirdre Barton and Wanda Winch,
    photo researchers; Karen Risch, product planning editor

Photo Credits
Bob Miller, 11
Bruce Coleman Inc./L. L. Rue, 14–15; Wayne Lankinen, 4–5, 12–13
Corbis/Raymond Gehman, 17
Creatas, 1
Kent and Donna Dannen, cover
McDonald Wildlife Photography/Joe McDonald, 19
Minden Pictures/Jim Brandenburg, 7; Konrad Wothe, 20–21; Mitsuaki Iwago, 8–9

The author thanks Barbara Nielsen of Polar Bears Alive and Dr. Andrew Derocher of the University of Alberta,
Canada, for their assistance.

Note to Parents and Teachers

The Animal Homes series supports national science standards related to life science. This
book describes and illustrates bears and their dens. The images support early readers in
understanding the text. The repetition of words and phrases helps early readers learn
new words. This book also introduces early readers to subject-specific vocabulary words,
which are defined in the Glossary. Early readers may need assistance to read some words
and to use the Table of Contents, Glossary, Read More, Internet Sites, and Index/Word
List sections of the book.

Word Count: 131
Early-Intervention Level: 15

Table of Contents

Dens

Bears sleep deeply during the cold winter. They sleep in dens.

black bear →

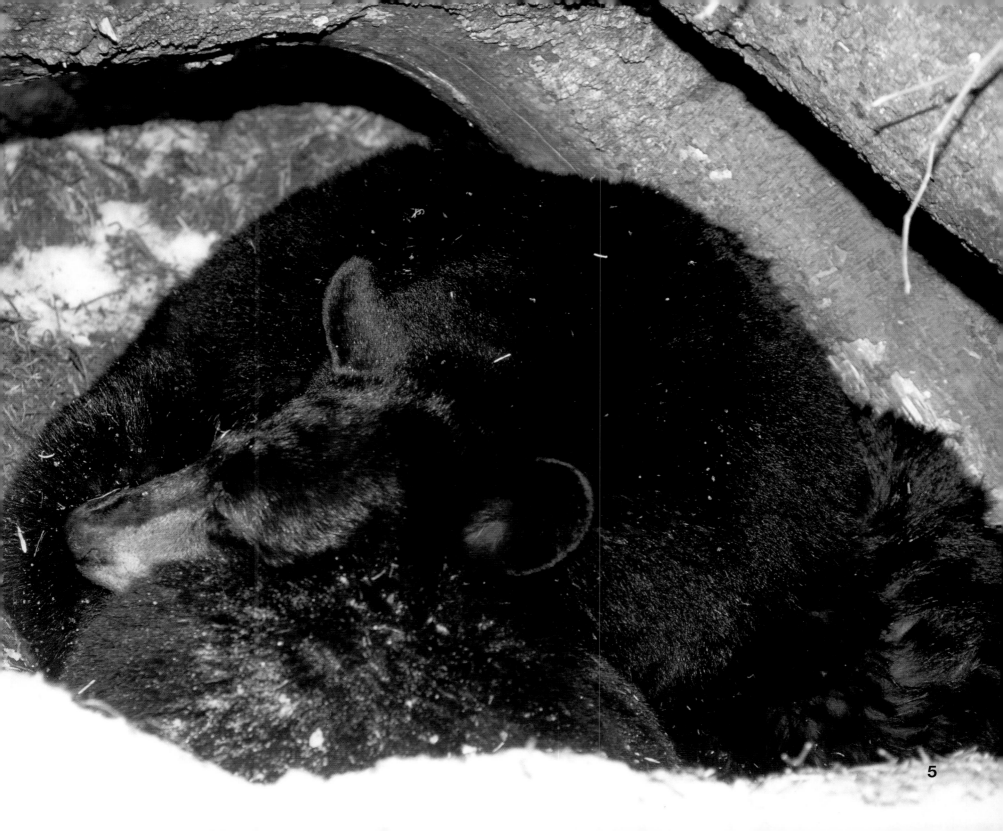

Bears make dens in hollow
trees, in caves, and under
large rocks. Bears sometimes
dig new dens in the fall.

bear den ➡

Most polar bears dig dens in the snow. Some black bears sleep inside hollow trees.

polar bear and cubs ➡

8

Some bears take only a few hours to dig dens. Other bears take several days.

grizzly bear ➡

Cubs

Female bears usually have
two cubs. The cubs are born
in the den.

black bear cubs ➤

13

Newborn cubs cannot see.
They have little fur. Newborn
cubs stay warm in the den.

grizzly bear cub ➤

Cubs hide safely from
predators in the den.
Cubs also rest in the den.

black bear cub ➤

Cubs grow quickly. They explore outside the den.

grizzly bear cub ➤

A Good Place to Rest

Dens are good places
for bears to rest and stay
warm. Bears and their cubs
leave their dens in spring.

grizzly bear with cubs ➤

Glossary

black bear—a kind of bear that lives in the forests of North America

cave—a large hole underground or in the side of a hill or cliff

cub—a young bear; two cubs usually are born at one time.

hollow—having an empty space inside

polar bear—a kind of bear that lives near the North Pole

predator—an animal that hunts other animals for food

sleep—to rest; some bears sleep deeply for several months during winter; some scientists call this sleep dormancy or hibernation.

Read More

Levin, Amy. *A Bear's Year.* Compass Point Phonics Readers. Minneapolis: Compass Point Books, 2003.

Tagliaferro, Linda. *Bears and Their Cubs.* Pebble Plus: Animal Offspring. Mankato, Minn.: Capstone Press, 2004.

Wilson, Natashya. *Bears.* My World of Animals. New York: PowerKids Press, 2004.

Internet Sites

FactHound offers a safe, fun way to find Internet sites related to this book. All of the sites on FactHound have been researched by our staff.

Here's how:

1. Visit *www.facthound.com*

2. Type in this special code **0736823816** for age-appropriate sites. Or enter a search word related to this book for a more general search.

3. Click on the **Fetch It** button.

FactHound will fetch the best sites for you!

Index/Word List